better together*

*This book is best read together, grownup and kid.

 akidsco.com

a kids book about

a kids book about

CHANGE

by David Kim

A Kids Co.
Editor Jelani Memory
Designer Duke Stebbins
Creative Director Rick DeLucco
Studio Manager Kenya Feldes
Sales Director Melanie Wilkins
Head of Books Jennifer Goldstein
CEO and Founder Jelani Memory

DK
Editor Emma Roberts
Senior Production Editor Jennifer Murray
Senior Production Controller Louise Minihane
Senior Acquisitions Editor Katy Flint
Acquisitions Project Editor Sara Forster
Managing Art Editor Vicky Short
Publishing Director Mark Searle
DK would like to thank Shahroo Izadi

This American Edition, 2024
Published in the United States by DK Publishing
1745 Broadway, 20th Floor, New York, NY 10019

A catalog record for this book is available from the Library of Congress.
ISBN: 978-0-7440-9903-4

DK books are available at special discounts when purchased in bulk for
sales promotions, premiums, fund-raising, or educational use. For details, contact:
DK Publishing Special Markets, 1745 Broadway, 20th Floor, New York, NY 10019, or SpecialSales@dk.com

Interested in inviting David Kim to speak at your school?
Visit: **TopYouthSpeakers.com**

Printed and bound in China

www.dk.com

akidsco.com

This book was made with Forest
Stewardship Council™ certified
paper – one small step in DK's
commitment to a sustainable future.
Learn more at www.dk.com/uk/
information/sustainability

For my daughters Skylar and Zoey.

우리 사랑하는 하늘이와 마음이에게.

Intro
for grownups

You may be wondering why we should talk about change.

Well, change happens all around us. We experience it every day. It's a big part of life!

Every change comes with a loss and the birth of something new. If you move from one city to another, this change comes with the loss of seeing old friends, but also the gaining of new ones.

If we don't give our kids opportunities to explore and process change, their fears and frustrations could come out in unhealthy patterns such as shutting down or being unable to calm themselves. There are also changes that are certainly worth pausing for and celebrating, and this acknowledgement can be so meaningful to kids.

I hope this book will provide a space for you and the kid you're reading with to slow down and address any questions and uncertainties around change!

Hi, my name is David.

I probably haven't met you, but I know for a fact that I have something in **common with you**.

Do you know what that is?

CHA

That's right!

Change is something that happens to everyone, no matter

how old you are,

where you live,

or what you do.

(Don't forget to turn the book again!)

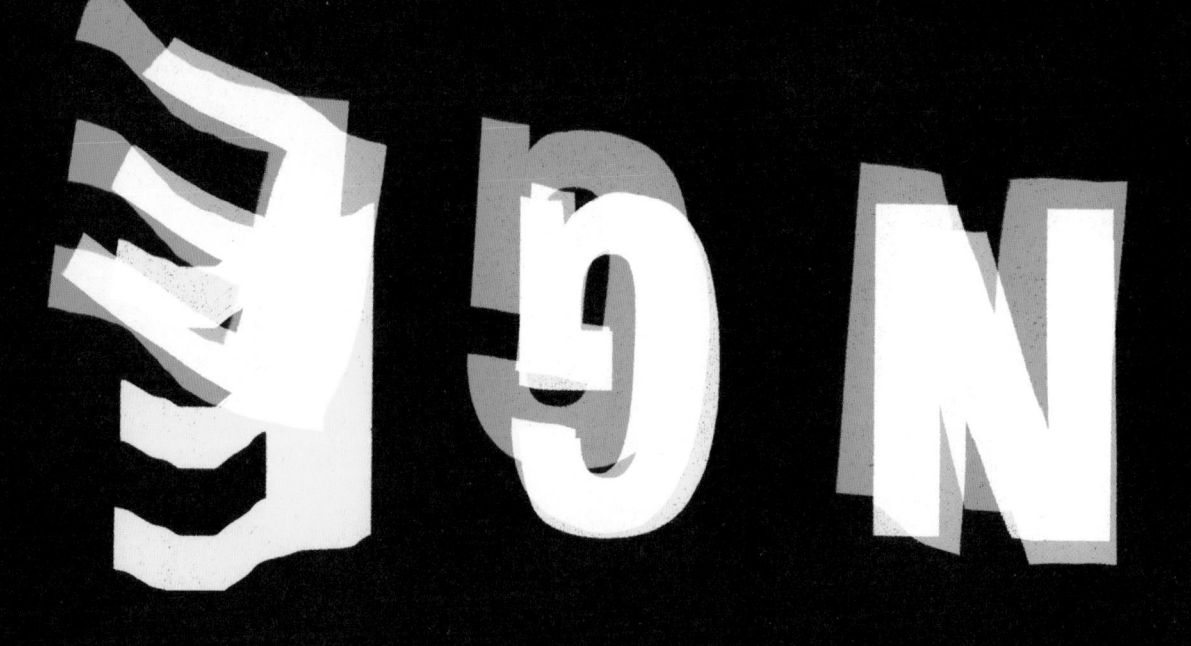

When I was 10 years old,
I moved from my home in
Korea

to New York City in America.

This meant a lot
of changes, like.....

Language.

In Korea,
hello looked like this:

But in America,
hello looked like this:

Food.

In Korea,
lunch looked like this:

But in America,
lunch looked like this:

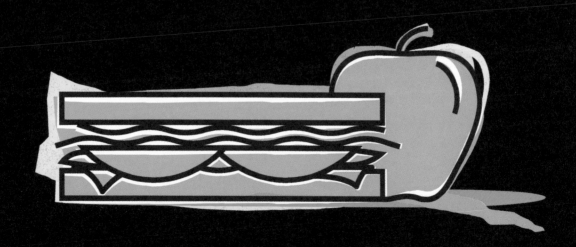

Names.

Back home, friends had names like this:

은혜, 민준, 권우, 태훈...

But in America,
friends had names like this:

John, Ashley, James,
Grace, and Emma...

To be honest,

so many things **changed** when I moved that I can't even remember all of them.

Even though change is something we **all** experience, I've noticed that people don't really talk about change a lot.

Change is something that happens **so much** we sometimes don't even notice it's happening.

Sometimes *change is* something you

CHOOSE.

Like what you will wear,
who your friends are,
or what to read.

But more often *change is* something that happens **TO YOU.**

Like moving, what school you go to, or getting sick.

Change can be really hard to describe and understand, but if I had to say what change is, exactly, I'd say...

Change is when something becomes different.

When something goes from being one thing to another.

Try reading that one more time.

Because so much change
happened in my life
all at once...

I was scared.

After the first week of school, I didn't want to go back.

Because I didn't have any friends.

I would sometimes eat my lunch in the washroom.

That way, I wouldn't have to sit alone in the cafeteria.

Some of my classmates would make fun of the smell of my Korean food,

so I started eating bagels and pizza for the first time.

This change wasn't so bad because I ended up liking bagels and pizza! But it still wasn't easy.

Some of my classmates couldn't pronounce my Korean name.

Try pronouncing "Jang Hyun."

They laughed when they couldn't do it and I was embarrassed.

It's pronounced "JAH-ng HY-eon," by the way.

So I gave myself an English name that would be easier for them to say.

I told everyone to call me...

David.

Have you changed *your* name because people couldn't pronounce the one you were given when you were born? If you haven't, can you imagine what it might feel like?

It seemed like everyone wanted me to change who I was and what I liked in order to fit in.

I wasn't sure where my
place was in this new life.

Fast-forward: I'm here writing this book, and everything worked out for me in the end. But before I tell you about that, let's talk about you...

What's something that has changed in your life recently?

Maybe it was moving to a new desk in your class.

Or maybe it was moving to a new city like I did.

When that change happened, were you...

scared?
excited?
overwhelmed?
happy?
surprised?
angry?
sad?
disappointed?
Or not sure what to feel?

Change can make us feel
lots of different things
at the same time.

It can be **hard** at first. Especially with an unexpected change. Because you're taken by SURPRISE.

And, even when a change **is good**, it can take some time to **feel good**.

That's just because we're not used to it yet.

Now, when change happens,
we might do **1** of **3** things.....

1. We **resist** change by fighting against it.

I told my parents I hated school
and never wanted to go back.

2.

We **ignore** change by acting like nothing happened.

I didn't share how I really felt.

But I bet you already know that neither of these will make the change any better!

So, it's good we can do the
third thing instead...

3. Embrace change.

That's what I decided to do eventually.

I made new friends but still kept in touch with all my friends in Korea.

I started eating pizza and bagels, but I still enjoyed galbi and kimchi.

I embraced my new name, but was still OK with being called Jang Hyun.

Do you know what
can make change easier?

WHEN YOU CAN TALK ABOUT IT AND SOMEONE LISTENS TO YOU.

For me, this was my teacher, Ms. Strawtuly..........

I remember her patiently
and kindly answering
my questions.

I also remember her labeling each item in the class in both Korean and English, just for me.

It made me feel understood and cared for.

when **change** happens,

what can **you** do?

Find someone who is trustworthy, and **tell them** about the change and how you feel about it.

It might be a parent, grandparent, aunt, uncle, sibling, teacher, friend, or coach.

Someone who you think is a good listener.

It's really **OK** to talk about change!

You can start by saying things like:

"I am worried about..."
"I am excited because..."
"I am scared to..."
"I am looking forward to..."

It's also **OK** to ask for help to deal with change!

All you have to say is:

"I need help with..."
"I need help with..."
"I need help with..."
"I need help with..."

Just noticing it
and talking about it
may seem small,

but it could make things **A LOT** easier—and even fun!

And remember, change is something that happens to **everyone**.

YOU'RE NOT ALONE!

So, can you think of any changes that you would like to talk about?

Why not start right now?

Outro
for grownups

Understanding and navigating change is difficult for children and grownups alike. But it's inevitable and we don't have to go through it alone!

Here are 3 suggestions for navigating change:

1) Talk about a recent change that has affected you personally. How did you feel? How did you cope with it? What did you learn? Allow your kids to see that it's OK and safe to process change and the emotions that come with it!

2) Sometimes your kids might not want to talk about change, and that's OK! Just remind them that you're available to talk about it and answer any of their questions when they are ready.

3) When your kids do decide to share, it's important to not underreact or overreact. When you respond in this way, you are not honoring their experience and feelings. So, instead of reacting, take time to consider your response and how it might affect your kid!

About The Author

David Kim (he/him) is a husband, father, author, and pastor in Silicon Valley, California. As an immigrant kid to the USA from Korea, he navigated many unique changes. This is the book he wished he'd had growing up.

Change can be hard, but some changes are worth celebrating. No matter what, life is full of small and big changes, and this book is meant to be a bridge—a safe space for kids and grownups to process how a change may be impacting their lives.

 @davidjanghyunkim  @davidjanghyunkim

Made to empower.

 a kids book about racism — by Jelani Memory

 a kids book about ANXIETY — by Ross Szabo

 a kids book about DISABILITY — by Kristine Napper

 a kids book about IMAGINATION — by LEVAR BURTON

 a kids book about belonging — by Kevin Carroll

 a kids book about failyure — by Dr. Laymon Hicks

 a kids book about GRATITUDE — by Ben Kenyon

 a kids book about LIFE ONLINE — by Dave S. Anderson & Blake Fleischacker

 a kids book about body image — by Rebecca Alexander

 a kids book about IMMIGRATION — by MJ Calderon

 a kids book about EMPATHY — by Daron K. Roberts

 a kids book about GENDER — by Dale Mueller

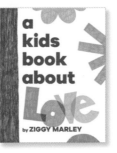 a kids book about Love — by ZIGGY MARLEY

 a kids book about EQUALITY — by BILLIE JEAN KING

 a kids book about MONEY — by Adam Stramwasser

 a kids book about FEMINISM — by Emma McIlroy

 a kids book about adventure — by Dr. Ben Tertin

 a kids book about CLIMATE CHANGE — by Zanagee Artis & Olivia Greenspan

 a kids book about CONFIDENCE — by Joy Cho

 a kids book about BEING NONBINARY — by Hunter Chinn-Raicht in partnership with The GenderCool Project

Discover more at akidsco.com